Mandurian Stories

By You

The People of Mandurah

Edited by Xanthe Turner
Published by Turner Books
Supported by Shape Mandurah

Copyright © 2019 by Turner Books.
Cover design by Xanthe Turner.
Compiled and edited by Xanthe Turner.
All rights reserved.
Published by Turner Books, Mandurah, Western Australia
ISBN 978-0-6484303-1-5
No part of this publication may be reproduced, distributed, or transmitted in any form or by any means, including photocopying, recording, or other electronic or mechanical methods, without the prior written permission of the publisher, except in the case of brief quotations embodied in critical reviews and certain other noncommercial uses permitted by copyright law.
For information regarding permission, please contact Turner Books.

www.turnerbooks.com.au

Mandurian Stories

By You

2019

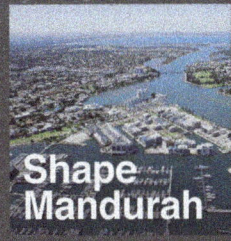

Created for Mandurah,
by Mandurah,
with the support of
Shape Mandurah

Foreword
Nanci Nott

Xanthe Turner began planning this anthology early last year, inspired by her love of Mandurah, and the people who live here. Shape Mandurah breathed vital life into the project, and Mandurian Stories was born.

In an early call for submissions, Xanthe said:

"I want everyone in Mandurah, regardless of age or ability, to have an opportunity to express themselves."

Xanthe envisioned an anthology which would "represent Mandurah as a whole, through snapshots of the individuals who live, work, and play in our beautiful city."

Xanthe shared her vision with our community, and our community shared back.

Mandurian writers, artists, and children collaborated to create a tangible manifestation of the creative spirit of Mandurah.

The words and images in this book contain fragments of lives, facets of experience, and apects of unique understanding. The common thread, woven through each page, is a deep-seated appreciation for Mandurah itself.

Our collective love of this beautiful city binds us together like pages in a book. We are all collaborators in the figurative anthology of life.

Every Mandurian deserves immense recognition for the time, passion, and effort involved in creating Mandurian Stories.

Nanci Nott
28th May, 2019

About the Editor
Xanthe Turner

Xanthe Turner has lived in Mandurah most of her life. She is passionate about her community, the environment, animals, books, and art. Xanthe is rarely seen without a sketchbook, and her natural habitat is the zoo.

In addition to writing, illustrating, and publishing books, Xanthe is working towards an Arts degree online, and is currently undertaking an art internship with Mandurian artist, Cindy Wright.

Xanthe plays guitar and piano (not at the same time) and her life goal is to befriend a sentient robot.

Photo credit: Veronika Sajova Photography

MANDURIAN

Dr. Louise Helfgott

Jo Gliddon-Baker

Annette Pesek

Julie Watts

Sarah Cole

Mary Ann Rath

Estuary Guardians Mandurah

Mandurah Dolphin Rescue Group

Michael Gorman

Kevin Lindsay Fowler Th. C. (Hons)

Mandurah Historical Society

Claire Cavanagh

Hannah O'Keefe

Karen Blake Rowe

Gail Willems

STORIES

Nikky May

Maddy Mac

Caroline Julian

Isabella Robinson

Amelia Kathleen Willis

Chase Williams

River Williams

Isabel Cummins

Hailey Cummins

Bonnie Cunningham

Aaron Gwynaire

Nanci Nott

Azalia Turner

Xanthe Turner

Veronika Sajova Photography

A Night on Long Island
By Dr. Louise Helfgott

There is something very primeval and peaceful about an estuary. Especially in the dim light of twilight as you row out into the still water, using only manpower to guide the vessel towards a distant island. Pelicans, seagulls and cormorants inhabited the island for their nesting grounds but now they hovered behind the boat expectantly. It was a wonderful fishing spot; the waters flowed rich with thick schools of yellow-eyed mullet and cobbler and after a hard evening's work, the soft shores of the island made a gloriously comfortable bed. Hence, although they were straining now with the effort of their oars, they did not mind for they were looking forward to the night's rest under the stars. Already, the faint twinkle of the Evening Star beckoned them to the West.

His partner, Lance was a taciturn man, given to long periods of sullen moroseness. Occasionally, he would dispel this image of himself and play a joke on an unsuspecting child, but for the most part he remained remote, almost aloof, drowning in his moods. Neither of the men were married, but while he could envisage himself with a family in a few years' time, he could not imagine, try as he did, his partner in a similar situation. It was not that the man was devoid of charms; his rugged, tanned face could even be considered handsome. However, he had never exercised these charms with women, seeming to prefer his life of solitude. Archie contemplated him now, remembering him as a child, often the loner on the edge of other childrens' games.

They had known each other since they were small, although Archie was a few years older and thus had the clearer memories of his partner. Still, he did not mind Lance's quietness on these fishing trips. It gave him a chance to reflect on the beauty of the estuary at night and lines of poetry would filter through his thoughts. When it was time to haul in the nets, Lance proved his resourcefulness then and all doubts Archie may have once had about him were cast away along with the undersized fish, the "cackers" as they were usually called.

Now, Archie glanced at his partner as they both strained hard on the oars. A silvery glow reflected from the rising moon illuminated his drawn features and he seemed more tense than usual.

"Anything wrong?" Archie enquired casually.

"Nuh." The answer had a finality that ended the brief conversation.

Even if something was wrong, Archie knew he could not wedge it out of his partner by further questions. So they rowed in silence while the sky grew darker all around them and a cool breeze played with their hair.

They would camp that night on Long Island and with the first light of morning, rise to set and haul in their nets. Although happy with most aspects of his work, this was the part Archie loved especially; sleeping under the stars on a warm summer's night beside a camp fire. Already, he could taste the billy tea and smell the potatoes roasting on the hot coals. He rowed harder and Lance responded with some extra strong heaves also.

Alongside the channel leading to the banks of Coodanup, they paused to consider the view of a few, isolated fishing boats scattered like toys on the still water.

"What about we try in there for a change?" Archie suggested, knowing full well what his answer would be.

"Nuh," Lance responded definitively. "Too many boats. Won't be any good fish left for us."

Archie smiled to himself. He knew perfectly well from past experience that Lance would have declined even if there weren't any boats in the channel. Then, his excuse would be "Nuh! It's be full of boats if it was any good." He had resigned himself to the fact that if he wanted to fish off Coodanup, he would have to do it by himself which is exactly what he had done many times. For a young man, Lance was already set in his ways and difficult to budge from his routine habits.

The sky was now completely black, except for the pale glow of the Milky Way above them and the silvery, gold glow of the moon rising over the dark escarpment in the distance. It was now too shallow for them to continue rowing and so they scrambled out of the boat into the water that gently lapped over their leathery skin. It was midsummer and the estuary retained the day's warmth much longer than the wide ocean.

They waded into shore with the boat drifting up and down behind them. The sharp tips of shells wedged between their toes and etched tiny wounds on the soles of their feet but they hardly noticed them, so used were they to walking over all kinds of terrain. They hauled the boat high above the water line, taking into account the tide. Once they were confident the boat was secure, they set about gathering twigs and dry branches to light a fire. The moon provided enough light for them to rummage through the patchy bush beside the beach and it only took a few minutes to gather a substantial load of fuel.

"You got the matches?" Lance asked.

"Nope. Thought you were bringing them."

Archie stopped stacking the wood momentarily to dwell on this new turn of events.

"Oh dear, looks like we will be rubbing sticks." Lance grinned to himself.

"That will take forever if we can get it going…" Archie searched through his pockets frantically.

Lance waited a moment longer to enjoy his concern and then produced a box of matches from his pocket.

"Seems like I had 'em here after all," he observed, smiling.

Archie flashed him a quick, bright grin and said, "You had them all along, didn't you? Thought I could rely on you." The interjection of humour lifted their spirits. Soon, they had a blazing fire crackling and spitting sparks onto the sand. When the first eager, intense flames had died down, they unpacked their bags and threw some potatoes onto the hot coals to roast. After awhile, they added some steaks to barbecue. They ate their food with relish when it was cooked, their appetite stimulated by the hard work and fresh air.

Contentedly tired, they stretched out, using their elbows to support their weight and looked out over the dark water, now broken by a silver road connecting with the moon. In the distance, a chorus of crickets chirped furiously and the occasional croak of frogs added to the entreaties of mountain ducks and teal, banishing the stillness of the night. Archie breathed deeply, enjoying the warm seabreeze. Although he came from a small town, he still loved the solitude of the deserted island. It gave him a feeling of expansiveness, as if by merely breathing, he could encompass it from end to end. It belonged to Lance and him and the birds, of course. It was now a part of him, just as the nets, lines and old fishing boat belonged to him. He could not imagine life without them.

Lance rolled over to face him, the moonlight adding a certain mystery to his handsome features.

"Should be a good haul tomorrow," he mumbled.

"Yes," Archie agreed. "Always seem to catch more on these sorts of nights." He was surprised at Lance's attempt to converse. Usually, the man would lie for hours in silence rather than say anything. Maybe something was wrong, after all.

"Been doing anything lately?" he asked casually.

"Nuh!" Lance replied emphatically. "What's there to do?" he added almost defensively.

"You might want to come to the dance with me, one of these days. Some nice girls go there."

"Nuh!" Lance looked away into the distance, his eyes had a misty, faraway expression. "Don't want a nice girl."

"What about a not so nice girl?" he joked, but it was lost on Lance who had drifted away into his own thoughts.

Archie was now sure something was bothering his partner but he could not decide what exactly it might be. He racked his brains, trying to recall everything that had happened to Lance recently. Then he remembered there had been that girl Lance had seemed to like. Archie had seen him talking to her a few times in the town and he remembered thinking how animated he had looked. He remembered reading in the local newspaper that she was recently married someone else.

Maybe that had upset his partner. He perused the other man's face again searching for clues but his expression was cloaked with blank indifference now.

Archie turned over to lie flat on his back so that he could look at the stars. There was no point saying anything further while Lance had that shut-off expression and besides, he wanted to enjoy the clear panorama of constellations and galaxies above him. He knew the brightest stars and could easily recognise the Southern Cross and the Pleiades or Seven Sisters as it was commonly called. Mars glowered red on the horizon, noticeably different from its companions. He wondered about the future and whether people would walk on its red shores one day. Even the moon seemed to send out an invitation, luring his attention to its deeply cratered face. One thing he was certain about, it would not be him who would go. He had not travelled further than one hundred miles yet and had no desire to either, preferring the familiar landscape of his home town, Mandurah best.

As a child, his parents had insisted he finish high school in the city, fifty miles north of Mandurah but he had insisted just as emphatically that he was staying. He had won in the end. The life of a fisherman had drawn him in with its promise of freedom and open vistas and now he was caught, tangled up in its tantalizing nets forever. He yawned. Although it was still early, gauging from the position of the stars, the rowing and fresh, tangy air had tired him out. He cast another glance at Lance who was lying perfectly still now, a Mummy in his remoteness, and then closed his eyes. They had dug small holes for their hips to nestle and he sank further down, nuzzling into the earth's warm shoulder. The soft sand blew lightly over him but he no longer noticed. Everything had become a warm, hazy blur…

***

Day broke to reveal a colourful, misty horizon. Red and indigo streaks pierced the mist, spanning out from a turquoise band of light that paled against the dark expanse of water. Everything seemed to have a dream-like quality, that morning. They were already awake, having been stirred from their deep slumber by a kookaburra laughing from the swamp oaks in the distance. Too often, they had been fooled by the magpies cajoling through the night and now they responded only to their more trusty indicator of morning. Eager to be out again on the estuary, they quickly rekindled the fire and prepared a billy.

After breakfasting on warm toast and tea, they blotted out the fire and packed their meagre belongings into the boat. Soon, they were rowing out to a suitable spot to launch their net.

Archie momentarily ceased rowing and Lance, as if on cue, hauled himself from the boat into the cold, clear water. He untangled the perimeter of the net from the stern of the boat and grasped it firmly in his hands, while Archie rowed tracing a broad circle. The sun's first beams were breaking through the haze, suffusing the ripples generated from the boat's movement with a golden glow. Sensing the bounty to follow, swarms of cormorants and seagulls hovered above the boat. While Archie rowed, the net was being drawn out into the water and the heavy lead weights lining the edge dragged it down to the sandy depths. Meanwhile, the light corks on the other edge held the net upright in the water; an invincible and invisible cotton prison to the unsuspecting, yellow-eyed mullet that swam head first into the mesh.

When Archie completed the circle, Lance leapt back into the boat and then with both of them standing on either side of the aft-thwart, they hauled in the net with slow, deliberate movements. When they reached the fish struggling in the mesh, they deftly extricated them, flinging them into the bow of the boat. After awhile, their movements seemed to fuse together in one continuous flow and all that could be heard was the swish of the net being drawn in and the clunk of the fish striking the boat's hard, wooden floor. Neither noticed the writhing bodies of the mullet as they twisted and turned spasmodically, their tails flailing wildly against each other. Their stunned expression slowly glazed over as the men continued working, oblivious to the dying surrounding them.

"Good haul today, Lance mumbled approvingly.

"Yeah. A real, decent haul," Archie agreed.

After a while, he paused in his work and pulled out a shotgun from the bow of the boat. He aimed it at a cormorant swooping down at the net and fired. Suddenly, there was a great flutter of wings flapping furiously and the swarm of birds ascended in one coordinated flurry.

"Catch their own fish, they can," he muttered. "Don't see why we have to feed them, too."

He returned the gun to its resting place and then surveyed the wonderful, wide vista of the estuary. The deep colours of the sky had faded and now the low sun hung like a golden balloon, its warm rays dancing on the small waves. The soft splash of water against the boat and the birds chorusing from their nests in the spearwood trees on the island formed a musical symphony that floated all around them. Soon, the sun's rays would be intense but now the cool brilliance of light washed the world with a magical, mystical wonder. Archie breathed deeply and tasted the slightly salty water. One of the oars fell from the seat and clanked loudly against the floor as the boat gently rocked…

***

He woke to the loud banging of someone knocking at the door. At first, he thought it was the oar banging against the bottom of the boat but then he realised he had been dreaming. His body ached a little as if it had been engaged in hard, physical labour and this further reinforced the sense of reality of the dream. He rubbed his eyes and stretched, then slowly hauled himself out of bed, all the while calling out, "Just a moment. Coming."

He shuffled into the lounge room, with its high, blue ceiling and walls decorated with flying ducks. The door was a little stiff to open but he gave it a hard yank and released the catch.

"It's you, Ben. Good to see you. I was just having a nap." He greeted the tall, young man who waited casually on the verandah.

"Sorry to wake you. I just came by to drop you off some fish."

Ben handed him a plastic package exuding a strong aroma of fresh mullet. He was immediately launched back into his dream.

"Mm. Fresh mullet! I was just dreaming about them." Archie smiled appreciatively. "Thanks. Want to come in for a moment?"

"Just a couple of minutes then. I've got to take a load of cray bait over later." Ben made himself at home without any further invitation. As Archie's godson and regular visitor, he felt quite at home in the fisherman's house.

"I was just dreaming I was fishing on the estuary, hauling in the nets like in the old days with Lance. Camping overnight on Long Island. What a wonderful life it was!" Archie called out from the kitchen as he stored the fish in the refrigerator. He returned to the lounge room.

"The camping came to an end when I got married in 1950. But even though Lance never got married, he wasn't too keen on camping on his own. He got too used to sleeping in his nice, soft bed. Things were so different then."

"Yup," Ben agreed.

"How's work going? Catching much?" Archie asked.

"Oh, it's been real slow lately. Had to sign up for the dole for the last few months. It's been like this every year now. Only good time is the prawn and crab season."

Archie shook his head remorsefully. "It was different in my day. No such thing as the dole. You had to work hard when the fish were around and save some money for the bad times. But then we used to fish at night and by the morning we'd have lots of boxes of lovely, fresh mullet just waiting to be sold. Trouble is, you fellas don't want to work too hard now, that's all."

"It's not just that. There's no money in mullet anymore. Only use for 'em is as cray bait," he said emphatically.

"I don't know about that. I look for them all the time in the supermarket but I can never find them. Nothing better than a nice, fresh mullet for dinner."

"Anyway, the estuary's all clogged up now with all that algae and muck. Scares away the fish, it does."

"Scares off the fishermen as well," Archie suggested, cheekily.

"It's awful. Smells rotten, it does. Can't be too good for anything. All those chemicals and fertilizers," Ben added defensively.

"It was better in the old days, that's for sure. The mullet were nicer than any old crab or prawn any day. Hmm! Wish I was out there fishing." Archie drifted off momentarily.

Ben rose and looked around, a little impatiently. "Well, better go now. Got some work to do."

Archie saw him off but his thoughts weren't with him anymore. He was remembering the old days when Lance and him were hauling in the nets on the estuary, watching the sun rise in the distance and hearing the cry of a swooping cormorant as the mullet lashed against the sides of the boat in their last death throes.

'A Night on Long Island'
was previously published by the
Mandurah/Murray Arts Council, and in FreeXpresSion.
It is published here with permission from Dr. Louise Helfgott.

Dr. Louise Helfgott

Louise received an Australian Postgraduate Award and Edith Cowan University (ECU) Research Excellence Award to complete her PhD in Creative Writing after being offered scholarships at both Murdoch University and ECU. 'Frames', written as part of her PhD, was short-listed in the national Playwriting Australia competition in 2010 and 2011 and was produced by Class Act Theatre with a two-week season at the Subiaco Arts Centre and a week at the Mandurah Performing Arts Centre in May - June 2014. "Frames" is currently shortlisted for publication by Currency Press. Louise won the Magdalena Prize for Feminist Research in 2013.

She has written numerous plays, poetry and stories. Most recent credits include productions of Whispering Leaves (2015 Yaburgurt Reference Group, Mandurah), The Body (Pocket Theatre, Perth, 2008), The Bridge (Mandurah Little Theatre, Mandurah, Kwinana and Bunbury, 2006 and Mandurah 1997), A Closer Sky (Mandurah Little Theatre, Mandurah, 2004), Estuary Dream (Stretch Festival, Mandurah, 2002), Diathesis (Nanasus Productions, Melbourne, 1998). Light in her Eye won the Todhunter Literary Award for Drama (2014) and was staged at the Perth Fringe Festival in 2018. A Closer Sky was nominated for an Australian Writers' Guild award (AWGIE award) in 2005 and other plays have been shortlisted in the Short and Sweet Festivals in Melbourne and Sydney (2007, 2008, 2009, 2011). The Bridge was a finalist in New Musicals Australia in 2011. In earlier years, she had a play workshopped at the Australian National Playwrights' Conference (1979) and was the youngest playwright to be selected at the time.

She had a book of poetry 'Can You Hold the Sun?' published by FreeXpresSion, New South Wales, in 2004. Her book 'Thistledown Seed' was shortlisted in the Dorothy Hewett Awards, 2018. Louise's play Potchnagoola, commissioned by the Katharine Susannah Prichard Centre in Perth will be staged on 5th and 6th October 2019 as part of the 50th anniversary commemoration events.

Dawn Patrol

Lined up like soldiers , the surfers stare out to sea.

Their feet wrapped in the cold sand. Later hoards of beach goers will skip, hop, and shuffle,
across the burning surface.

A light salty mist kisses Charlie's cheek and he breathes it in like a promise that he will soon paddle out.

"There's a few lines," one of the hopeful soldiers announces.

Hoodies off, wetsuits up, zzziiiip.

A dog taking his owner for a walk snuffles by heaving on his lead.

Charlie stretches and squats like a frog poised to launch into the water.

The sky is a hazy golden glow. The air is thick with salt and anticipation.

His leg rope fastened he makes his way to the water, the icy foam lapping at his feet.

He lunges onto his board , his arms cutting through the chilly water as he paddles out.

Once in position Charlie sits on his board,
feet dangling
staring out to the horizon like a salute to the ocean
and a prayer for waves.

A lump billows under and past him.
Then another, the swell growing.

His patience is tested as a wave surges forward
and he paddles furiously,
he is on the crest and then retreats suddenly,
backwards, foam flying.
Too soon.

Back he paddles more determined,
more focused...

This time.

Sucking,
heaving,
the wave rushes toward him.

Paddle, paddle, paddle.

The wave connects, they are one.
He stands, feeling the power behind him.
He carves across the face and up into the rolling white water.
Floating across the top
then dropping down.

Charlie rides almost into shore but flips off the back
exhilarated, exhausted.
He is alive, he is one with the wave.
The soldier, the ocean warrior.

He is at peace.

Jo Gliddon-Baker

Frogmouth Sings

By Jo Gliddon-Baker
Artwork by Annette Pesek

Past Autumn Glen
At the end of Winter Drive
Stood an old gum tree
Right outside number five

From dawns first light
Through early morning hue
The suns beams danced
To illuminate the dew.

Way up high in the branches
On a gnarled old burl
Sat a frog mouth , eyes closed
Quite content with the world.

Two magpies flew past
With a mudlark behind,
Trying desperately hard
To be one of their kind.

They swooped and they snickered
"get a load of that guy"
then they worbbled and twittered
and flew right on by.

The frog mouth stood stoic
Not a flinch or a flutter
But stood , quite heroic
Not a sigh , not a mutter.

A galah came to rest
He stared at the frog mouth,
And although quite perplexed,
Said nothing and flew south.

Birds came and birds went
Wattle birds, doves.
Some laughed or made comment
Some poked and some shoved.

But the frog mouth stayed still
And kept his eyes closed
Ignoring with will
All the teasing imposed.

Major Mitchells flew over
Squawking with pride
At how attractive they were
And how the frog mouth should hide.

But after sunset,
Under veil of night,
As all other birds settle
And abate from flight

The frog mouth awakes
And puffs up his chest
With poise and with grace
He is now at his best.

Oooom oooom oom ooom
He sings... and then
Oooom whooooo oooom whoooo
He sings again and again.

In the tops of the trees
Where the other birds nest
His song rises and weaves
And puts all to their rest.

Ooooom ooooom oooooom
Ooom whooooo oooom

Oooooom oooooom oooooom
Ooooom whooooo oooooom

Jo Gliddon-Baker

About the Author

My name is Jo Gliddon-Baker. I am a wife and mother of three boys, and reside in Dawesville, Western Australia.

I am a Teacher Assistant and work in the early years area. I am passionate about children's literature, oral language, and storytelling. In the past, I have worked as a children's entertainer and storyteller.

I grew up in the Midwest town of Kalbarri where I was inspired by the natural beauty, flora and fauna of the area.

In 2006, I self-published a small children's picture book, 'Bulgie Meets a Thingamabob:
A Fable from Flummery Forest'.

Currently I am in the process of publishing a picture book called, 'Petrichor – the smell of rain' through Maggie Dent.

All proceeds of that book will go toward drought relief.

Annette Pesek

Annette Pesek has lived all her life in Melbourne and has recently moved to the Mandurah area.

She has been drawing and painting as a hobby since she was old enough to hold a pencil and paintbrush. Upon completing a Maths/Science Education degree at Melbourne University, she attended watercolour classes with Melbourne based realist artist Walter Magilton. However after a few years she turned to Botanical Illustration, as she discovered that this was her true passion. Since then, she had attended regular classes with the well-known Melbourne based botanical artist Terry Napier, until she moved to Mandurah.

Top left: 'Gum' by Annette Pesek
Top right: 'Oak leaves' by Annette Pesek

Bottom left: 'Gumnut flower' by Annette Pesek
Bottom right: 'Cherries' by Annette Pesek

In the past, Annette has sold her work at group shows (such as Rotary Art Shows), via commissions and through word-of-mouth channels.

Her works have also been displayed at the Melbourne Royal Botanic Gardens' by selection only "The Art of Botanical Illustration" and also the "Natural History" exhibitions. One of her paintings was also selected to represent October in their 2018 Botanical Illustration calendar.

Annette has three daughters, helps run her family's food business, does interior design and colour consulting and also does administration work for companies on an ad hoc basis.

Now that she's moved to Mandurah, she intends to devote as much time as possible capturing the beauty of the local flora/fauna and also WA wildflowers in her paintings and drawings.

Left: Annette Pesek

The Push and Pull of Fishing

the thrill   as his catch
breaks surface

the pang   of it in his hand
the silver shiver of its body

as he bends low   into his deed
removes the hook like a child's splinter

the Easterly pushes against the estuary
(all blue muscle and shadow)

lines flung west   are dragged east
by the Dawesville current

on the rocks   the estuary leans
into the edges of afternoon

the lowering sun on the far bank emblazons
rooftops   covers them in Florentine gold

a fist of fish   a gasping bucket
an ancient crackle of campfire

the ocean leaps   into dusk
its lisp for mercy   all over the wet rocks

Julie Watts

Julie Watts

Julie Watts is a Western Australian writer and Play Therapist.

She has been published in National and International journals and anthologies.

She won The Blake Poetry Prize (2017) and The Dorothy Hewett Award for an Unpublished Manuscript (2018).

Her second poetry collection, Legacy, was published by UWA Publishing in November, 2018.

Summer Haunts
by Sarah Cole

MANDURAH, 1926

"There's a ghost in there," Harry said, with a child's conviction.

He pointed at the Peninsula Hotel, drifting on the edge of the inlet like a mirage. It was a grand, lonely thing built on a sandbar beside the Mandurah township, and accessible only by a fifty-metre footbridge.

Harry, David and Ellie were perched at the mainland end of the bridge, not daring approach any closer; earlier, the boys had been chased out of the Pen's beer garden by the publican for throwing snails among the tables till a swarm of seagulls had descended on customers.

"Bull," scoffed David.

Ellie whacked his shoulder. "Don't curse."

"Dad curses."

Ellie sniffed. "And I'll tell him you do too, when we go back to camp."

David scowled at her.

"It's real," Harry insisted. "The ghost. The ticket boy at the Hotham Theatre told me. He said there are rooms that are always cold, and odd noises at night."

"Perhaps it's the old Perth mayor who died there?" whispered Ellie, but when Harry turned to her in earnest, she laughed.

Around them, holidaymakers fished and crabbed and paddled in the shallows; children bragged about their hauls, families picnicked. Duck hunters' guns crackled in the distance. The bay was busy in the autumn time, when a caravanserai of visitors from Perth set down their shanty town of tents and horse carts and tin can vehicles. The three children were part of the deluge who'd travelled for miles to the Mandurah oasis. They were camped in an oiled wool tent in the bush to the north.

"There ain't ghosts," David muttered. He wandered in circles on the jetty while his brother and sister dangled their toes in the water. "Can we go somewhere else? I want to explore more."

"We explored the bay every year, David," said Ellie. She held a fishing wire, and lazily jiggled it in the water with one finger. "Sit with us."

David did not want to sit. The long journey to the coast by carriage on the unsealed Pinjarra Road had made him achy and stiff. He considered annoying Ellie by describing his sore arse.

"We haven't been far over the car bridge," he insisted.

Ellie and Harry peered at the sparsely wooded wetlands across the bay.

Harry said, "S'pose you're right!"

"Carn, I'm bored to bits here, let's go."

"Father said to stay near town," Ellie said. Their father's war-weathered leg had worsened enough to retire him from chasing up the boys, and he'd asked Ellie to be responsible for them.

"Ever since you started secondary you've been such a bloody bore, Eleanor."

Whack. She got his leg.

"He'll see us if we go over," she said. "He and Aunt Marlene are crabbing up there." She nodded to the north. David peered at the far southern shore, shaggy and wild and uninhabited, stretched intriguingly into the distance before dissolving into the light bouncing off the bay.

"Then we won't go that way," he said, and marched off.

Harry toddled after his elder brother, chattering excitedly.

Ellie was beaten. She sighed and followed. Perhaps she could prevent the worst of the trouble.

***

The pale, hot sunlight swelled down from the sky and pressed on their backs, and the glare was too strong to look anywhere but down. So they watched their bare feet skip across the wide wooden planks of the bridge; plunge into the pale shallows, scattering fish and crabs; make dents in the dark, marshy sand; pick careful paths through the twigs and serrated leaves as they entered the bush.

The children stayed in the shallows of the bush, keeping the glimmer of water always to their left. Time oozed by slowly with the ticking of cicadas. The boys teased crows, and poked things down potential snake holes, and competed to peel the biggest sheet off the paperbark. Ellie inspected banksia husks, with their many eyes, and hummed to keep at bay the creeping unease that always settled on her when she found herself in wild bush. It's quiet, she thought, and ancient and cares not a whit for you. She'd heard plenty of stories of the bush eating people up, leaving nothing so much as a bone to be found.

"What's that?" Harry asked.

He'd found the edge of a clearing. At the centre, a nest of corrugated tin sheets was rusting in the sand, littered with decomposing blankets and cooking utensils and a dusty fire ring.

The children hovered at the tree line. Nothing had attempted to grow near the ruin of the hermitage.

"I heard about this bloke," David said boastfully, breaking the silence. "It's his house I reckon, or was. He got spooked by all the dead people that washed up on the beach here fifty years ago and he went crazy and refused to cross water ever again."

"Who's the one with silly ghost stories, now?" Ellie said. But they stayed where they were.

Harry had gone still in a rare moment of focus. "What is it?" Eleanor asked, and Harry pointed. Nestled in a thick cavern of scrub nearby was a little wooden dinghy.

"Oy, there," David murmured, and then—giving the rotting hut a wide berth—dived into the scrub, clawing away the boat's leafy bindings and hauling it out.

"It has a paddle, too," Ellie remarked, plucking it from the bottom of the boat.

The vessel was hardly larger than a cattle trough; just enough space for two uncomfortable adults, or three gangly children.

Ellie allowed her brothers' gleaming eyes to coerce her into helping carry it to the water.

She was, after all, a child as well.

The sea breeze, cool and breathy, had rolled in earlier than usual from the nor'west. Ellie kept her hands pressed to her thighs to keep her cotton dress from taking wing, imagining herself blown into the sky. She scowled at Harry when he clambered gracelessly into the dinghy and splattered silt across the plank seats, but she sat on them anyway. The water clapped against the hull, giving little shoves of encouragement. David pushed them off and made an ungainly lunge into the space between his siblings. Their cries of annoyance were the only human sound around.

They curled in, knees tessellating, allowing the boat to drift in slow circles where it was willed by the lazy current and blasting wind. Mostly the water was only inches deep, with seagrass waving and schools of silvered minnows darting under the rippling pane of the surface. David prodded a suspicious blob with the paddle and it turned into a stingray and whipped out of sight. Loitering gulls paddled warily out of their path, eyeing them like gossiping villagers, and two pelicans watched their passage with an unperturbed yellow gaze. Harry shrank back when one yawned, its rubbery throat billowing wide.

The dingy rocked the children into a daze. The wash of warm sunshine and breezes unfurled them like wilting flowers. David drooped his wrist over the edge and dragged patterns in the water with his fingers. His hand soon went limp as he dozed.

It was only when cloud stole over the sky and cooled the air that Ellie roused, and recognised the traffic bridge as a thin blight on the horizon of sprawling wetlands.

"Oh, dust." She snatched up the paddle from Harry's lap. "Wake up." She prodded them with it and then began to slice the water, trying to steer for shore. Harry stirred reluctantly, staring heavy-lidded up at the sky. David helpfully dumped a handful of water on his face.

"Stop, stop!" screeched Ellie, as Harry nearly tipped David overboard. "You're making this impossible!"

"You're a lousy sailor, Ellen." David snatched the paddle and stroked the water—pulling them in a wonky circle.

It occurred to them all at once that they had never had control of the boat. The single paddle was impotent in their hands.

They peered around for land. It was a struggle to determine where the water ended, with the shoreline blurred by floating swamps. The water they drifted upon was fathomless, veined with foam, a flat steel colour in the grey light.

Harry made a panicked sound.

"There now, don't fret," Ellie said.

"I can't swim, Ellie," Harry said feebly.

"You won't have to, just be calm," Ellie said, thinking of her own poor ability. They'd learned in a billabong, and had never had to contend with a current.

"Look," David said.

Over the tops of the trees to the east peeked the edges of a windmill's white sails.

"Help!" hollered Harry.

"Help us!"

Ellie saw the mooring post of the mill, isolated from the shore by a wide tidal influx. It was badly chipped, wrapped in frayed rope and lichen. "Nobody's been here for a long time," she said. "No use in shouting."

"We can't be sure," David snapped. He took the paddle in both hands and stabbed it into the current. The boat lurched and swung in a circle, and his siblings gripped the edges, white-knuckled. David's face scrunched into a red wrinkle of determination as he ploughed against the water, elbows in the air. Murmuring encouragement, Ellie watched her little brother throw his entire, meagre weight into the task. Each stroke grew clumsier than the last.

She glanced around frantically. She could not even see the bridge anymore. *We're going to be washed out into the bay and lost.*

She did not show how frightened she was. "Harry," she said levelly, "I'm in the middle and can't reach, but could you grab that?"

He looked where she pointed, at the mooring post standing sentinel to the mill. The dinghy had pulled quite close to it.

"I think so," he said.

The boy hung out of the boat and scrabbled his fingers on the ropes. For a moment Ellie thought he'd lose grip—but then his arms went around and he hugged it to his chest, pulling the boat with him.

Ellie patted his back and praised him. David dropped the paddle in the boat and slumped over his knees, arms shaking.

Ellie took one of his hands. "You did so well. Rest, and I'll figure something out. Harry, hold on there, don't let go. We mustn't be swept away."

Ellie took the paddle and held it by the very tip, dipping it experimentally into the water. When it touched nothing she withdrew it hurriedly, spooked. She hugged her arm to her chest as the wind wrapped around her wet sleeve and chilled her. She met David's wide eyes; with all his bravado gone he looked awfully young.

"It'll be alright," she said.

Grumbling, Harry was trying to rearrange his grip on the post, and suddenly made the boat tip. "Harry!" screeched Ellie, then screeched louder when he slipped, and his skinny legs were pulled out of the boat. Ellie and David went spinning away, shouting. Harry locked his arms around the post, clinging for his life.

Ellie reached for Harry, but they were already too far away. David took up paddling again in earnest.

"Don't let go, Harry! Hold on!" Ellie cried, but she could see him slipping. The ropes were loosening. His bare feet scrabbled. She saw a drop of blood run down his arm from a ripped fingernail.

They weren't moving closer. Her arms stretched out but the space did not close.

Harry slipped.

He disappeared under with hardly a splash, and the water gave a satisfied burp.

David made a short, horrid sound of alarm, but Ellie was knocked windless. The roar of panic that had filled her head was muted. She was oblivious to David's efforts to turn the boat, and sagged with her arms in the water, staring at the spot that had swallowed her brother. He was drowning and she was powerless to reach him.

A bedraggled head popped above the surface.

Now Ellie screamed. She didn't want to watch Harry die but she could not move her eyes away.

He turned to them with an oddly smooth, quick motion, and held his arms up.

"Ellie! David!" he called.

They gaped.

"I can stand!" he said, his chin lapped by waves.

Ellie dived out of the boat. Her dress mushroomed around her chest, blinding her for a moment. She felt her feet touch a silky sand bed and kicked. The cotton dress dragged and tangled around her, and she struggled through it, hiccupping and sobbing, crashing through the water and throwing her arms around Harry. His skin was icy.

They pushed together through the water towards the shore. A splash behind them told her David was following behind them. When they reached the shallows, kicking arcs of water around their legs because they were too weak to lift their feet higher, they sagged. Ellie toppled over and sat in the mud, holding Harry in a tight hug. She was freezing, but her face was hot from crying and she beamed like a lunatic.

David fell to his knees next to her. He lobbed the paddle into the swamp.

"Bloody hell," said Ellie.

David looked at her with a grin and cursed filthily. He had silt smeared on his face and his sodden shirt hung off him like a tent. She wanted to laugh.

Harry hadn't made a sound, but she could feel him vibrating in her arms, perhaps from fear, or cold, or shock. She tried to squeeze it out of him.

The children huddled together, feeling the muddle settle around them, and watched the abandoned boat as it was borne off across the bay, headed for the wilderness.

The End

All artwork accompanying Sarah Cole's, 'Summer Haunts', was created by Annette Pesek, except for the black and white image opposite, which was created by Izzy Orloff, is owned by the State Library of W.A., and was submitted by Sarah Cole.

Author's Note
Sarah Cole

This story, Summer Haunts, was inspired by several events, and folklore in the Peel area.

The original Peninsula Hotel was indeed rumoured to be haunted, although it didn't stop it being a popular picnicking and drinking spot for patrons that cam from all over the state.

The traumatised hermit may not have existed, but the poor people washing up on Doddi's Beach after the wreck of the James Service did, in 1878.

There is a tale of an immigrant worker who'd accidentally found himself out of his boat and clinging to a mooring post for dear life, thinking the water was deep enough to drown him. When he let go from exhaustion, he realised the water was only several feet deep.

Then there was the horrible event of the Herron siblings' boating accident on Lake Clifton in 1886, with two of the four drowning and the others clinging to the overturned boat for days.

The Bush Hermit of Mandurah

Written By Mary Ann Rath
2018/19
For the Archival Project

The Hermit Hummingbird
flies and hovers
One hundred Heleconias
are ritually visited daily

The solitary hermit has hundreds of thoughts
and questions wanting to find an answer
and has a habit of eating meagre food

In 1966 the Mandurah Mail,
the local media
gave a man a label, a title:

"The Mandurah Bush Hermit"

He routinely went
from cottage to cottage
to find and make
a place to sleep and eat

Six months of,
a diet of baked beans
and beer

"Someone has been sleeping in my bed!"

"In my holiday shack!"
chorale the locals...

"Even the frypan has been used
on the carpet in the lounge,"
was a whinge,
"to cook baked beans!"

"We think he gets in through the windows!"

Women working in the cannery were advised,
"Do not leave your children alone at night,
while you are at work."

The hunt began, to catch the hermit.

In earnest, a trap was set.

Six months later...

Constable Butt, with his band of merry locals,
discovered the hermit's hideaway for that day.

They grabbed Robert Alexander Cruikshank,
and took him away

The cavalier, Robert, exclaimed:

"Thank God that is over!
Have you got a cigarette?"

Then the whispers, rumours, speculation, and gossip
began amongst the locals:

"You know that bush hermit,
Robert Alexander Cruikshank,
the one in the Mandurah Mail?"

"He is a Vietnam veteran,"
was heard at the local RSL,
"and has shell shock."

"He is a homeless person,"
discussed the men,
dragging the prawn net in the Estuary

"Yeah he was traumatised at Tardin,
the boys home
and has been unable to relate to people."

"He ran away from his wife and children,"
was discussed at the CWA,
"It was just too much for him
after Vietnam,
when he slept, he would remember a struggle
and act it out."

"He had an accident at work,"
remarked someone at the cannery,
"and he never recovered from hitting his head."

"He had a mental illness,"
voiced a man
at the Brighton Hotel bar,
"and couldn't hold down a job."

He was taken away...

Mary Ann Rath

Mary Ann Rath considers herself as a conceptual artist using various mediums to express an idea that she hopes to articulate to the audience.

Usually the idea is of an environmental or social issue.

Mary Ann had an art practise even though working as a trained nurse as she taught children in the public system on the virtues of kindness, sharing, and the Jesus stories, through song, puppet plays, drama, and storytelling.

Now that Mary Ann has retired, her practise has broadened to express ideas in the visual art scene with paintings, sculpture, upcycling, and verse.

Mary Ann was captivated by a story in the archival files in the Mandurah Museum that of Robert Alexander Cruikshank.

Why he was hunted down got Mary Ann thinking of the reasons why Robert did not have a home of his own.

The questions to ask are: was he homeless, was he unemployed, kicked out of home, a Vietnam veteran, had a mental health issue or was it a choice?

Also to use the label of a bush hermit required an examination. A hermit is a type of humming bird.

She doesn't think it was Robert's choice to be homeless,
as his words upon capture were,
"Thank God that is over,"
and he asked for a cigarette.

Mary Ann is forever grateful for a roof over her head.

Left: Photography by Mary Ann Rath
Background: Photography by Azalia Turner

The Story of Low Blow

Low Blow is a dolphin you will see a lot in town waters, so do keep an eye out for her, if you are between the new bridge and the ocean.
Low Blow is pretty easy to recognise by the notches in her dorsal fin.
She definitely caused a stir in 2015, when she had her calf, Benji.
She was in the media quite a lot with this beautiful little calf.
The cruise boats would see her almost every day with her new baby.
We hope Low Blow has many calves to come.

The Story of Hayley

Hayley is a female adult with a female calf called Comet. Hayley was named after Hayley Dodd, as a tribute.
Hayley stranded, with her male calf, on the twenty-fifth of November, 2014, at the very furthest point of the Harvey Estuary.
They were high and dry on the beach, where it was unlikey they would be seen, let alone rescued.
Luckily, a passing plane (or helicopter) saw their bodies on the sandy beach, and reported them.
The Watts are a long-term fishing family down in the Harvey Estuary. They have a boat which is able to go into shallow water.
We asked them to take us to these animals and rescue them.
We were really lucky to have the assistance of the Watts family.
We were able to save Hayley, although she was very sunburned, and it took months for her to heal. Hayley now has white sunburn, very visibly, on her body. I'm happy to say that Hayley (and her most recent calf, Comet) are happy and healthy, and you will most likely see them in the Harvey Estuary.

Left: **Hayley**
Right: **Low Blow**
Images (and permission for use) courtesy of **Estuary Guardians Mandurah.**
Audio stories by **Mandurah Dolphin Rescue Group.**

Memories of Mandurah - A Nostalgic Dream
By Michael Gorman

When I think back to my childhood, I become instantly drawn back to those early memories as a kid spending many a weekend or school holidays at the 'nostalgic dream' that is Mandurah.

The fondest, are that of the King Carnival on the western side of the Mandurah foreshore. An ageless amusement park, that even today still conjures up feelings and memories of a simpler time.

A day in Mandurah was not complete without a visit to Kings Carnival. My grandparents would bundle my siblings and I into the car - an esky filled with sandwiches, cakes, and cans of lemonade - and off we'd go to Mandurah for the day.

I remember, as young kids, my brother, two sisters and I, would burst with excitement when we would look from the car window and we could see the giant ferris wheel turning in the blue, cloudless sky, a welcome sign the carnival was open for the day.

Upon arriving at Kings Carnival, we would run straight for the Dodgem Cars. Then it was on to the Teacup Ride, the arcade games, and finally, the ferris wheel. I can still remember that rubber smell from the bumper cars, the creak of the ferris wheel, the background noise of the arcade machines, and the childish laughter of my brother and sisters.

I only hope Kings Carnival will keep its old world charm, and continue to create the joyful memories that I experienced as a child, for future generations to come.

Michael Gorman

Michael Gorman is a qualified horticulturalist living with his lovely wife, and two year old son in Lakelands, Mandurah.

Michael grew up in Rockingham, and as a child would spend many a weekend in the sleepy holiday town of Mandurah, having very fond memories of visiting Kings Carnival and fishing with family from the old traffic bridge on Mandurah foreshore.

Mandurian Childhood in the Nineteen Fifties

My family and I came to Pinjarrah (and then Barraghup), in 1950. Like Pinjarra, Barragup has had the 'h' removed from it's name by people who don't like to leave things alone.

Most children at this time had jobs to do before and after school, which included bringing in the firewood for the wood stove, collecting the eggs, milking the cows, and chasing the sheep out of the bush paddocks.

In the winter time, you also had to break the ice off the water troughs to let the stock drink.

There were no indoor bathrooms, laundries, or toilets. You bathed in a large tub on the kitchen floor, with hot water coming from kettles heated on the wood stove.

Light came from kerosene lamps or candles. You read, or did your homework, using these.

Heating was from a large wood fireplace in the lounge room, or standing in front of the stove.

The telephone was attatched to the wall, and you listened to a large wireless (radio) for entertainment. There were no miniature radios, TVs, computers, or mobile phones, and there were definitely no fast food places!

Every house had a backyard with a chicken run (for the eggs, for baking); a vegetable garden; and an orchard, for fruit.

Bread and biscuits were home-baked. Butter, jams, and sauces were all home-made.

Fruit was bottled and preserved for use throughout the year, and you made your own clothes.

People were mostly self-sufficient, catching fish, crabs, and prawns, and shooting kangaroos (which were plentiful and disease-free) to supplement the diet.

Excerpts from 'History of Mandurah and Life Between 1950 to 2017'

Written and compiled by

Kevin Lindsay Fowler Th. C. (Hons)

Mandurian Memories: Reflections of Mandurah

One of my first reflections of Mandurah was Christmas, 1951, when a sea-plane came in over the Peninsular Hotel, and landed in the river.

At this time, there were no walls along the foreshore, the land went straight into the water. A boat on the shore was rowed out to the plane and a man in a red suit got out. They rowed him back to shore, where he climbed a two metre ladder to the top of the bandstand, where a very large chair and a Christmas tree were placed. This bandstand was where the toilets on the foreshore are currently placed.

The first live theatre was in our large barn at Barraghup, in 1952. The actors and actresses used the garage for their change-rooms. The audience sat on stools in the middle of the large room.

Many happy hours were spent at these performances.

However, at one of these, so much noise and banging was going on, a carpet snake came out to investigate. This cleared the main room, and no one would return until the snake had been removed.

The first movie theatre was a tent beside the Capitol Hall on Pinjarra Road, where Mr. Edwards showed movies.

In the early 1950's, the land along Lakes Road (from Fowler Road to the Murrayfield Airport) was unfenced property. The virgin bush was full of kangaroos and brumbies (wild horses).

In the 1950's, you could buy half an ice-cream cone for threepence, or a full cone for sixpence. Icecream was expensive, because it was something only eaten on special occasions, unlike today, when it is eaten nearly every day.

Excerpts from 'History of Mandurah and Life Between 1950 to 2017'

Written and compiled by

Kevin Lindsay Fowler Th. C. (Hons)

To a True Friend

Kevin Lindsay Fowler Th. C. (Hons)

My love for you has grown slowly like a flower.
First a seed, planted in fertile soil,
Then the roots, to give nourishment;
Slowly the stem grew in strength,
Followed by the flower of loveliness.

The fragrance of the flower is to remind you
That like the seed,
My love is deep and growing in fertile soil.
Like the roots, my love is giving nourishment,
To the stem,
Which is providing the strength to uphold this love
Which is showing forth in the glorious colours of the petals.

As the flower blooms forth
Into a most glorious display,
A masterpiece of rich beauty and splendour,
So my love blooms forth to enrich this beautiful friendship.

Image: Azalia Turner

Dryness

Kevin Lindsay Fowler Th. C. (Hons)

Looking out over the paddock,
After months without rain,
The dead grass stands stark,
With only a few trees,
Showing signs of green.
The ground is loose powdery sand,
Rising as dust whenever the wind blows,
And the gumtrees flower,
As the water level drops,
So that they may produce seeds,
To sprout when the rains finally come.

Image: Xanthe Turner

WAR MEMORIALS

The first War Memorial in Mandurah was a very large limestone rock placed on the Eastern Foreshore behind the change sheds opposite to Smart Street. This had flagpoles either side of it. It was moved to the front of the new RSL Hall on Pinjarra Road of the tenth of April, 1952.

The second War Memorial was on the second of October, 1981, when the clock tower in the centre of the roundabout at the western end of Tuckey Street was installed. This has recently been moved.

The third War Memorial was built on the eighth of January, 1988, on the western side of the river, near the old bridge, at the junction of Leighton Road and Old Coast Road. The base was demolished on the ninth of April, 1996, to make room for the Mary Street roundabout. The plinth was removed and resurrected on a new base on the corner of Third Avenue and ANZAC Place, and named, 'The Rose Garden Memorial'.

The fourth War Memorial was built at the Dolphin Pool. This War Memorial was built behind the Tourist Bureau. However, there was not enough room for veterans and participants, so it was decommissioned. The top was removed on the fifth of September, 2002, and it became a Garden of Remembrance Memorial.

The fifth War Memorial was a temporary Memorial set up on the Eastern Foreshore whenever a commemoration service needed to be held. This was in front of the Bandstand at the end of Gibson Street.

The new Mandurah City War Memorial on the Western Foreshore was officially opened, consecrated, and dedicated on the eighteenth of April, 2005, as the sixth War Memorial.

WRITTEN BY
KEVIN LINDSAY FOWLER TH. C. (HONS)

Left: Kevin Lindsay Fowler, 1966

Right: Kevin Lindsay Fowler, 2019

Mandurah Historical Society

Photograph provided by Claire Cavanagh

The Black Eyed Girl
By Hannah O'Keefe

I heard the slight tap on my door, a rhythmic and consistent tapping that could just be heard over the sound of my television. I carefully looked over to my wooden door, the greyish green walls surrounding decorated in a way that seemed to make it appear more predominant to my eyes. I felt my face scrunch into confusion at the sound.

'I don't remember inviting anyone over?' I thought to myself, as I stood from the battered chair of my apartment. Before walking over however, I mentally battled myself. Would I really want to answer it? On one hand it could be my neighbour asking for something or maybe my friends stopping by without asking once again, but on the other I don't want to be bothered with small talk.

I sighed audibly. I figured I should try to be a nice person to whoever felt the need to ask for my attention. I placed my feet into my slippers sitting near my chair and carefully walked to the door with tired eyes.

As I got closer the knocking seemed to echo through my small living room, as if it was coming from the inside rather then out in the hall. I slowed my pace as the door got closer to me, as the wood was face to face with me I completely stopped. A strange sense of panic came over me as a lump formed in my throat.

Why would someone be here so late?

I felt my breath pick up as my heart followed suit. Thats when it hit me, I was being absolutely ridiculous! This was an apartment complex, tonnes of young adults and teens lived here. Of course people would be walking through the complex throughout the night.

Hell, I'd spent many nights wandering through the halls trying to make it back home.

I shook my head at myself and chuckled at my over reaction. I placed my hand on the door knob and turned the handle. I heard the click and went to open my door. I stopped again, however.

With the curiosity biting at my brain I let the door close again and instead turned my attention to the peep hole. To ease my anxious mind I decided that taking a look would be the best idea, not really having any expectations.

As I stood on the tips on my toes, my neck craned like a baby chick waiting to be fed. The dirty, curved glass of the peephole framed my eye. It created a window of magnified curiosity, as my emotions poured from my eyes over the threshold of the door.

Kneeling on the carpeted floor was the cats killer; a little girl. The girl's attire a pale gathering of flowing fabric that balled onto the floor at her small frame, her ashy brown locks nearly met the fabric as her head hung low, her arm suspended in the air. Sobs flowed to my ears from the close proximity.

The sight of the girl knocked me back to my senses. God, I was an idiot! I mentally cursed myself. My nerves got the better of me, and I nearly left some kid all by themselves. I quickly opened the door where the girl kneeled, her arm still suspended as if ready to knock.

I felt myself close the door slightly. "Hey, what's wrong?" I asked slowly, peering around the wooden frame.

The child's brown strands covered their face as they spoke softly in a disconnected voice that flowed through the air as if she was right next to my ear.

"I need to use your phone, mister," she said, unmoving.

For a second I wondered if she'd spoken at all, or if my mind was playing tricks on me. I shook my head once again to get the airy feeling from my mind, cloudy and intense. A headache crept into the back of my head but I ignored it.

"Why, are you lost?" I asked while moving my body from behind the door, with a face full of concern.

"Please mister, I need to use your phone. Let me in, please."

An uneasy feeling settled in my stomach at the way she spoke. It was like speaking to a bot, a bot with only a handful of words in its program.

I shook my head a little, knowing something was off. This wasn't right at all. None of this felt right.

I made a split second decision to satisfy my conscience while getting the hell out of there.

"Go back downstairs to the front office there's a phone down there." I closed the door.

As I walked away, I realised I hadn't locked the door. I went to slide the metal latch shut, hoping the girl had left, sparing one last look out the peep hole.

After seeing the girl's face I felt better locking the door on her. I felt much better.

I turned up the television when the banging began.
I ignored the screaming from behind it.
I ignored the inhuman voice that surrounded and suffocated me.
I ignored the child with her brown locks, old dress, small frame and tear-stained face.
The tears that fell from those black, lifeless eyes penetrated my psyche as I slept away in my bed.
Just waiting for the moment where no doors or walls could stop it from meeting my gaze, with the abyss that lurked under her innocent form.

The End

Hello, my name is Hannah O'Keeffe.
I'm a 15-year-old Australian artist who enjoys writing as a hobby, with ambitions of becoming a professional artist and one day produce my own project(s).
I'm currently working on my schooling and plan to follow through with art in university.
I'm grateful to be a part of this fantastic project and am so proud of the community that came together to make it.
Thank you for reading a little about me, and have a good day!

Beacon of Light:
A Metaphorical Autobiography
By Karen Blake Rowe

The mist descended rapidly like a veil falling down her face, covering her eyes, blurring her vision. A cool dampness swirled at her feet and a rising uneasiness clasped at her heart. She knew intuitively that this wasn't the normal seasonal fog often known to shroud these hills at certain times of the year. For one, this wasn't one of those times of the year and two, this didn't feel normal at all and every cell in her body agreed.

It seemed only moments before that her heart had been filled to overflowing with the beauty of the meadow through which she had been wandering. She still carried the scent of the wildflowers and drying grasses on her clothes and the incessant chirping of insects and birds still rung musically in her ears. These moments which she stole alone in the hills have always enchanted her; exhilarating and freeing. These hills felt like home to her, familiar, warm and secure.

But now, as she began stepping through the first hem of trees cuffing the meadow, she suddenly felt a million miles from home. How did things change so quickly, so dramatically? She had not seen it coming. It seemed implausible, impossible, surely? Her fleeting confusion was quickly replaced by the urgency of fear and foreboding. She wanted to get through this shadowed patch of forest and continue quickly on her now familiar path and get back to her busy day. It would be patiently waiting, just as it always did, for her to return.

With each cautious step, an even colder blast of air would billow from under her feet. The mist became a dense fog; the air now thickened and damp. It suddenly seemed difficult to breathe. Her movements became heavy and laboured. Time seemed to have been fractured for everything had slowed. Each step felt like one hundred steps, each breathe possibly her last. She was being swallowed up in a fierce gathering storm and the fear she had sensed previously now squeezed tightly around her heart.

Her reasoning mind tried to rescue her; it kept grappling with what was unfolding around her. But the darkness began to cloak her; it weighed heavily upon her body and muddled her mind.

She could not fathom how, what had begun as a normal day, was now almost instantly anything but. The path ahead was visible in her mind and within herself she knew she could find her way through the familiar forest; she'd hiked this path so many times before. Instead the path became mysteriously elusive, seemingly floating away with the wind that was now chasing her down the hill. Feeling detached from reality, it was if she had entered a dream, her dream or her nightmare, either, with an unknown director.

***

He had noticed the signs for some time now, an accumulation of anomalies seemingly insignificant alone. It is so often in hindsight that a pattern emerges. He chided himself for not adding it up sooner; perhaps he could have been more prepared. Then smirked at his arrogance, for how could he possibly have known what coming, any more than he could have prevented what was happening now, before his eyes. His gaze was transfixed on the hills above, his pulse suddenly deafening in his ears; a panic struck him. Where was she? He knew she found solace in these hills and the morning had been so beautiful that he was sure she couldn't have resisted the calling of her sanctuary. She'd loved these hills since she was a child; she'd regaled him of so many of her tales, adventures and joys from those carefree childhood years.

He doubted that she noticed the signs, as he had. Her world had been busied with the having-to-do's of a mothering life. She was always pushing herself to do more, to be more. These traits had endeared her to him, for like her he too expected much from life. His thoughts drifted anxiously as he acknowledged to himself that lately he'd seen the signs of change within her too. Subtle as they were, he couldn't deny that her vibrancy had dimmed and that the child-like sparkle in her eyes had most certainly dulled.

But he couldn't dwell upon that now as his mind refocused on what was forming above him. There was a shadow looming down, an angry darkness consuming her beloved hills. Nature was about to have her say. There were no subtle signals to decipher here; a storm was gathering upon them, upon her. He had no chance of reaching her in time, of that he was sure, however he was still going to try. He raced upward, desperate to find her and gather her into him once more.

The air cooled quickly around him and clouds gathered at speed. He took a moment to glance back; he had hiked high enough now for his view to take in their home nestled blissfully in the still sunlit valley below. Such a vastly contrasting sight to what he was now fearfully watching engulf the hills above. A sinking realisation pained him; he loved her so deeply, she was his world. It was definitely too late to reach her now; she was in this unnerving storm alone.

***

She willed herself forward, her vision now blurred by rain, her steps unsteadied and her pleas for help silenced by the fury of the storm as it engulfed her. A deep roll of thunder grumbled loudly, so close it felt like a message from above meant just for her. There was no shelter, nowhere to hide. Not that she would stop anyway if there was; she needed to get home to her family. They'd be worried about her.

He'd know where she was on a day like today and he'd be out searching for her. This man, the one she felt safe with, enough to come home to, after living so many years away; he knew her so well. She hated the thought that she would have caused him to worry for her. Was this storm now upon them too? The children would be frightened. She was angry at herself for leaving them alone, it was her job to protect them, comfort them and assure them that everything was going to be ok. She wasn't there for them. Her heart pleaded silently for this storm to pass quickly.

Instead though, as the storm continued to rage around her, a vague numbness seemed to seep through her; like the medicating effect of alcohol as it enters your bloodstream. She noticed her heart harden slightly, not physically, emotionally. Was she simply steeling herself against the torment of the storm; a natural self-preservation response maybe? The dream-like detachment from reality that she'd noticed earlier had heightened. She could almost visibly see a wall being built around her; it couldn't be real, but it felt real. On the outside this wall shut out the wind, the cold and the blasting elements of the storm. But more, she could feel it inside and at a deeper level than she'd ever known before.

Awareness and a gradual realisation began to form consciously. This internal wall was protecting her from an inner storm; the complexities of her life. It corralled the endless soul searching, the nagging questioning of purpose and the innate self-analysis that could paralyse her at times.

Inside this buffering wall she could now see clearly the self-imposed pressures of her perfectionist nature, the lessening of self in her quest to please others and her intrinsic insecurities she so boldly hid from the world. It was if the storm outside was offering her a gift; a gift of insight or a gradual awakening of her true self. This gift was a beacon of light; warming her, guiding her. She chose to follow, trusting that it would lead her to safety.

***

Although we know that storms are temporary and that they come and go quickly, my metaphorical storm lasted well over a decade. Mystery illness swept over me seemingly from nowhere and stranded me without answers and without energy to cope with my young family life as I was fatigued beyond words, often bed-ridden and always brain-fogged. This illness robbed me of so many years, clouded so many memories and sadly, isolated me from many loved ones who were forced to watch helplessly from afar. Although now well on the road to recovery, the path to this point has had many twists and turns; it has been a very bumpy ride to say the least. I would not wish it upon anyone.

Upon reflection however, I am now at a point of gratitude, for my illness has taken me down a path I would not have travelled without it. I now have a very clear understanding of what it takes to recover from serious illness and how to live a healthy lifestyle. I have been able to guide my children back to this ancient wisdom that has been lost to us for several generations with the industrialisation of our food, agriculture and medicines.

Just as importantly I have been privileged to navigate an inwards journey that has realigned my life priorities, enabling a deeper depth of compassion for self and others and reinforcing a trust in life's processes. I am now a healthier, happier and calmer version of my old self and beginning to build a life again in a far more conscious state.

As you enjoy the many beautiful sunny days here in our beloved Mandurah, take a moment to think of the many around you who may be silently suffering their own version of a terrifying storm, with dark clouds following them, clouding their world to a point of despair.

Without judgement, be a beacon of light for them, for you just don't know when you might be the one seeking guidance yourself.

Karen Blake Rowe

Married, and mother to two beautiful boys, I've lived in Mandurah a little over ten years.

Eventually diagnosed with Chronic Fatigue and Severe Adrenal Fatigue, my illness has consumed most of my married life and all of my children's life.

Unable to work, I spent many hours researching and trialling ways to heal my body.

Current allopathic doctoring had no answers for my condition and I eventually found answers in the simple 'unscientific' art of correct diet and nutrition.

I am now mid-way through writing a book about what I've learnt so that others can prevent or heal from their chronic health conditions.

Statistics paint a very grim picture and show that we will all face one or multiple chronic health conditions in our lifetime.

Sadly, the correct information for healing is being withheld due to industry self-interest and government lobbying.

I hope to be a 'beacon of light in the sea of travellers', and ensure that I leave a legacy of Healthier Generations.

Email: blakerowe@iinet.net.au
Facebook: Healthier Generations

Gail Willems

Gail Willems is a retired nurse. She lives near the beach, swims, and plays with a body board. She drinks good shiraz... and the occasional bubbles.

Double Symmetry

Butterfly

Spirit of the land

Catching the first

Mornings Menu

Published in Prospect, Regime Books, Poetry D'Amour, Blackmail Press NZ, Kurangabaa, 5UV (Writers Radio Adelaide), Famous Reporter, The Mozzie, Creatrix, AquilleRelle (Belgium) dot dot dash, Long Glances, (Manning Clark House) Booranga fourW (Charles Sturt University), Idiom23 (CQUniversity Press), erbacce (erbacce-press UK), Dangerously Poetic (Byron Bay Writers Festival 2016), a poetry anthology, Adelaide journal (New York, Lisbon), Wild (Ginninderra Press) Heroines (Neo Perennial Press), and others. Haiku published and translated into Chinese. First poetry collection 'Blood Ties and Crack-Fed Dreams',
Ginninderra Press, 2013.

Spirit of the land

I read the scents of air like spars of sun
that swing in light and shadow on the wind
banksias flirt parrots skim cut and run
Swan river bends, edges grassed and sequined.

Benzene perfume sniffed across the highway
unseen it bleeds a darkness on the land
a spectre of the future where once lay
wild silence braced against the wind blown sand.

Waltzing up the incline of dry cheekbones
I unstitch night and loosen all the stars
untie the tides, their curl and crash long known
as night music, hums deep through traffic scars.

Long ago this Land stored power in daydreams
now Spirit woman mourns earths wounded streams.

Gail Willems

catching the first

The push of hips across a long flat board
a white horse plunges through a glass green wave
position taken as a silvered sword
engard and poised waiting to outbrave
the resounding barrage of water-hard
imagining the moment silence falls,
then in the bubble a soaring shard
sliced deep from an emerald, it calls
for a compelling all consuming ride,
knuckles clenched and white as any foam
I switch the grip and soar from side to side
in the long line of spume, I'm here I'm home,
but I can feel it coming back again
a thunder of ocean equestriennes

Gail Willems

Double Symmetry

Because morning cracks its light across the bay
beneath the shadow of the cliff   his gaze alters

Because en-point a wave rises in the mist   pirouettes
spins the bar
retreats to shore line's chorus   jettes across the bay

Because it resists gravity and time   rises in an encore
its renewed theatrics becoming one with air

Let there be dance

Because he creeps closer to navigate her whisper
willing belief to make impossible possible again

Because she spins in spiral colours
imprints the stage in a stop clench of heart

yrtemmyS elbuoD

Because the wave crest flaunts its solo run
splits the horizon in a slow fade

Let there be grace

Because it was a sound he heard thinned to transparency
threading the fabric of her going

Because he read the tune of the water   understood
how his dancer had folded her wings

Because her shadow space bordered the blue above
hung between sea and sky   leaving him to face the horizon

Let there be sorrow

Gail Willems

MORNINGS MENU

Look   through holes in the floor of heaven
light slants its way in fingernail increments
plays tic tac with the breeze   skims the skin of trees

Listen   pink and gray screeches duel blackarse crows
and punch drunk willy wagtails
the cranky call of a motor parts the salt swell of air

Look   waves crack and fall apart as they throw themselves
at a limestoned reef   a lone seal dances with a fish
and disappears in wave shore rhythms

Look   sand sucks each of our toes   softly letting go
the pinkness of pedicles   and tentacles
of a stray fisherman's night catch

Listen   I will gather a feast of sounds
heat them on a stove of words
pick this breakfast wishbone

Gail Willems

BUTTERFLY

kites fascinated you
coloured wings wet jewels
they flew with the light
the flip of the ocean
performed an incidental clowning
flicked aerostatic acrobatics

you cried out the flavours you could see
in a scouring sea a board detached
bobbed back to the surface
doing a hammer dance
wings trampled in the incandescent foam

you cried out the noises you could feel

away from here cocooned

a bone lattice mind
glitters in the white faced bolts
of electrocuting moonlight
stores in its rafters
the soft long cases of butterfly kites

Gail Willems

An Unexpected Move

Mandurah was the last place I ever expected to live. I have always been a north-of-the-river-girl, and moving south, especially this far south, was not even a consideration.

But unfortunately, I became ill and I could no longer work. This was during the time when Perth rental prices were ridiculously high. As a single mum, there was no way I could afford to stay in Perth while I wasn't working, so I had to find another option, a cheaper option.

That's when I began my search for somewhere further north, and Yanchep seemed like a good option for me. During one of my online rental searches (carefully selecting Yanchep and surrounds), a home in a foreign place called Dawesville popped up.

The house was hexagon shaped, so this caught my attention. Who wouldn't want to live in a hexagonal house? But I didn't have a clue where Dawesville was.

When I found out, I immediately threw out the idea. I couldn't move that far south. But Dawesville looked beautiful and I was intrigued.

The more I researched the area the more interested I became. It almost seemed like fate that this house popped up in a search nearly 150km away.

But my stubborn attitude put its foot down, the house was too isolated and too far from any schools.

My mind, however wasn't done with the idea and wouldn't let it go.

I came to the conclusion that it couldn't do any harm to just look. I began searching for houses in Dawesville, eventually coming across one that interested me.

The area seemed perfect and I decided that there's no harm in just looking at the house, I probably won't get it anyway.

I made an appointment with the real estate and drove an hour and a half to see this house.

The drive was difficult for me as I was still very sick, but I managed.

The house was average, however the moment I spotted kangaroos in the backyard I knew I wanted to live there. I filled in an application form and drove back to Perth. A few days later I got the call.

"Congratulations you have been approved for the house".

Without thinking I accepted it on the spot, well I guess now there's no turning back.

This was in 2014. My plan was to live in Mandurah for about a year, recover and then move back to Perth. I did recover, but didn't move back to Perth. I fell in love with Mandurah. The wildlife, beautiful beaches, relaxed lifestyle, and friendly people.

Mandurah inspires my writing and photography, and is the reason why I have gained back my health.

In Perth I never had the opportunity to experience the amazing variety of bird species, bandicoots and dolphins that Mandurah offers; or have kangaroos knocking at my door.

I also didn't have the pleasure of coming across some of Mandurah's more unpleasant wildlife species while in Perth. I hope never to find another scorpion under my bed, or a giant centipede in the spare room ever again! Thanks Dawesville.

I'm glad that I opened my mind to something new. If I had stuck with my stubbornness that north was my only option, I would never have found my home, and Mandurah is my home.

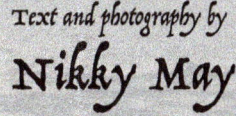

Text and photography by
Nikky May

Nikky is a writer, student, mum, amateur photographer and wannabe musician. She began taking her writing seriously in 2015. Beginning by writing free blog posts for various websites, and articles for a local suburb magazine. Eventually being a poor artist paid off and she was offered a position writing blog posts, SEO articles and website content for a Perth marketing company.

Nikky writes holistically about health, nutrition, wellness, mental health, science and spirituality. She is passionate about educating others through her writing and is beginning to write books which touch on the above subjects. She is currently completing post graduate nutrition after finishing her undergraduate degree in science and nutrition in 2013.

 Nikky May

Photography by Nikky May

Birds of Mandurah
Butterfly in my Backyard
Sunset on Dawesville Beach
Kite surfers on Avalon Beach
Gracie enjoying Dawesville Beach

Am I?

Molecular creativity

creating

of molecules

The electrical energizing

of molecules

metamorphosising

metastisising

metabolic

materialisation

the culmination

of

me?

Maddy Mac

Thought

Beast of burden, or willing dray
makes no parry
makes no break
days nor years
do the yoke erase
symbolism
by day
but the night ignites
subliminal insights

Tempt the human psyche
woven lead into darkness
sightless
muted outcry
homogenised
desensitised
all one
undone

The oxen, the beast
we are all
just more meat
butchered
and butchering
as our own fate
we recreate

A good time
for a little nail biting
then suck your thumb
it's just begun
You bit the quick
you lunatic

Maddy Mac

Join Our Cause

By Caroline Julian

Stop

Wait

Take a minute to enjoy your space

Isn't it nice not to be invaded
or
to be chased?

Take a moment to think

Does the existence of our whales
really need be made extinct?

Do you have to destroy
this beautiful creature of the sea
who enjoys swimming so gracefully
calmly through the waters
of the big blue ocean?

In its own space
just doing its own thing
not inflicting harm on anyone
not even thee!

STOP

Take a moment to think

Why does man treat me so?
Perstisting to chase, maim
or
even kill me?

Is it simply to satisfy his pleasures and needs
of making cosmetics
and dining on me?

Science, you say!
I beg to differ, please

Do you feel a sense of compassion?

And have no fear
to show you truly care

Like to show some emotion
even some concern?

Then

Please, please, please
feel free to join our great cause

of saving the whales

In return
all we can offer you
is a very simple

Thank you

Artwork: Aaron Gwynaire

ISABELLA'S JOURNEY

My name is Isabella. I am 12 years old and have been living in Western Australia since 2014. I love it here, and the journey over was more interesting then you would think.

Me, my two older brothers, and my mum attached our camper-trailer to the back of our car and set off. We were on the road again, driving from Queensland to Western Australia.

My mum was being driven insane from the very slow roadworks, the amount of people thinking it's amazing that she was traveling alone with three kids, and the VERY long journey to find a place that sells slushies for my brothers.

We were relaxing in the car, either watching a movie, or listening to music while looking out over the infinite red dirt landscape. Suddenly, my mum spoke up about how a check engine light popped up.

We tried to continue on until we found a better place to pull over, and oh, what a place we found.

We pulled over at the edge of the carpark of most cliché little service station I have ever seen. It was small, and only had two cars out the front. Two older-looking, cliché Australian guys sat out front at a table. A phonebooth sat at either side of the small building, and I swear I saw a tumble weed rolling past.

We walked into the cliché station, and it happened to be two rooms, one being a souvenir shop, and the other being a small room with tables and a front desk.

My mum talked to the guy who stood behind the counter for a while, while me and my brothers stood there listening. My mum tried calling for help, but there was (of course) no phone service. We instead tried the two phonebooths off to the side. One was broken and the other surprisingly did work.

After another hour of trying to figure out what to do, and how to do it, we still came up to a dead end. Someone could come out and get the car, bringing it to the next town, but we couldn't exactly go with it. Then we also had our trailer. The guy at the front desk offered us a room in the back to stay in but we obviously declined, because even if we were stuck out in the middle of the outback, with no idea on how to get to the next town, we weren't that helpless.

Suddenly, a guy who looked like he was just there for a small rest came up to us after seeing my mum obviously stressed. After explaining our dilemma he offered to help as he was also driving to Perth.

After even more time spent trying different things to attempt to fix the car, nothing worked.

BY ISABELLA ROBINSON

My mum went back into the building where she managed to get onto the phone with the front desk's corded phone.

Me, my brothers, and the guy helping us (who was called Tarek), all just sat there on the camper-trailer quietly awaiting any news from our mum, occasionally talking. After a while of waiting, my mum came out the door, slightly calling something out that we couldn't hear. After sitting there watching curiously, trying to determine what she was saying, the two cliché guys also started calling out. After more time spent, we ended up figuring out they were calling my eldest brother.

Tarek looked at my brother. "I think your mum wants you," he said simply.

My brother ran over, and we were (once again) left sitting there.

After more time spent waiting (and burning alive in the heat) we ended with the same problem as before. Some people were going to come out and get the car - bringing it to the nearest town to get fixed - but since we couldn't go with the car, we were stuck with the camper trailer. Suddenly Tarek spoke up offering the nicest thing. He offered to not only drive us to the next town, but also offered to take the camper-trailer the rest of the way to Perth as well. We were shocked at first at why, but accepted the kind offer. So we got our essentials out of our car, and reattached the camper-trailer to Tarek's car.

We drove another few hours until we made it to the next town, where we stayed in a cabin. The day after, me and my mum walked down to the car service shop and found that our car was fixed.

We left the small town, and in ten hours we made it to Perth, where we went and found our rental.

After settling in, we went and picked up our camper-van that Tarek drove over for us. After an entire year in Perth, we finally moved out to our newly built house, and only after a few years living in the place did I find out that a street only a few streets down was called the same name as the place we broke down at. Not only that, but a service station sits at the end of it as well, and if that's not destiny, I don't know what is.

Thanks so much to Tarek for getting us over in one piece, and with a care.

Because of that we now have a cool little story to tell.

I AM ISABELLA
AND I AM A 12 YEAR OLD MERMAID WANNABE!
I LOVE THE WORLD OF FANTASY,
AND I'M MAD ABOUT DOGS.

Mandurian

Left page: All artwork by Xanthe Turner

Right page: (Top to bottom) Xanthe Turner (bird), Azalia Turner (sunset), Xanthe Turner (building), Xanthe Turner (dragon), Aaron Gwynaire (fantasy beach), Nanci Nott (beach)

Art

Amelia

Willis

Amelia Kathleen Willis is a thirteen year old young lady, who is passionate about visual and musical art.

Amelia enjoys working with watercolours, graphite and charcoal.

She also loves singing, playing guitar, ukulele, and piano.

Chase Williams

Aged 7

River Williams

Aged 4

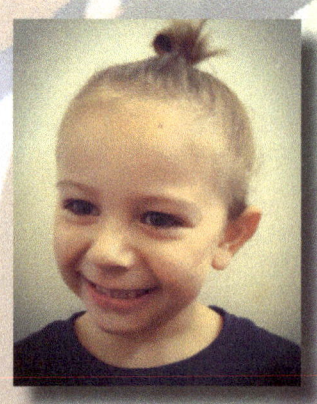

Hailey Cummins

Aged 9

Isabel Cummins

Aged 6

Bonnie
Cunningham

Bonnie is seven years old. She loves drawing, music, and gymnastics.

17 Reasons the Cult of Mandurah probably exists

1.
The majority of residents worship Mandurah as if it were a sentient being.

2.
The only people who say negative things about Mandurah
don't actually live here (I'm looking at you, Clarksonites).

3.
Halls Head is Mandurah. Dawesville is Mandurah. Meadow Springs is Mandurah.
Dudley Park is Mandurah. Silver Sands is Mandurah. Coodanup is Mandurah.
Greenfields is Mandurah. Falcon is Mandurah.
I could go on. All the suburbs want to be known as Mandurah.

4.
Could you imagine Leederville calling itself Glendalough? No.
But I'm pretty sure Leederville wants to be Mandurah.

5.
People quit travelling after arriving in Mandurah.

6.
I'm serious.
One minute, you're enjoying a spontaneous weekend away,
doing touristy things like watching dolphins,
riding camels, and eating crabs.

7.
Next thing you know,
you're living near the foreshore,
eating Simmos ice cream,
making friends with the pelicans...

8.
...and you know every estuary dolphin by name.

9.
We have more art galleries than prisons.

10.
Do we even have a prison?
Other than the one in the museum?

11.
That poor bushranger-mannequin.
He must get so lonely in his cell.

12.
I just realised, we don't need a prison
because the locals are all super-friendly,
and so are the museum staff. Yay!

13.
Despite being the second largest city in Western Australia,
you can't leave the house (not even to buy midnight milk)
without encountering six of your favourite cult members.

14.
But no one judges you for wearing pyjamas to the servo.
They too, are buying midnight milk, in their pyjamas.

15.
The secret password is 'Mandjoogoordap'.
Only cult-members know how to pronounce it correctly.

16.
If you can relate to this list, you may already be a cult member.

17.
If not, it's only a matter of time...

The Lonely Chair
Shortlisted for the Golden Pen Award, 2019
By Xanthe Turner

A lonely chair sits
in the corner of the room
legs rotting
as puddles of damp
soak into the forgotten wood
and the sad smell of mould
permeates the air

There was a time
when the house was full
of joy and laughter

A large family
sat around the table
each with their own
ornate chair

But now
the table is gone
and most of the chairs
are no longer there

Coldness emphasises
the void left behind
Warm conversation stopped flowing,
replaced
by the steady
flowing
of water
d
 r
  i
   p
  p
   i
  n
 g
   d
  o
   w
 n

the cracks in the walls
and holes in the roof
riddled with
peeled paint and mildew

First to go
long ago
were
the children's toys
replaced or thrown away
as they were outgrown
and then
even the replaced belongings
disappeared
when the children
grew up
and left home

Four chairs lost

The aunt saw no reason to stay
once her beloved nieces and nephews
had gone away
she'd always wanted to travel
so
she left the house
to discover the world
taking her bookshelf
and her partner
with her

two more chairs lost

Years flew by

one
by
one
the
rest
left
the
large
family
home

until

only one chair remained
memories engrained
in the sturdy frame

In her nineties
the last one
passed away

The family came
swarming back
like magpies
desperate for a piece
to remember her by

briefly
wonderfully
magically
the house was
rediscovered
filled
with joy and cheer
as they remembered
and reminisced
about the
happy years
they'd spent
together

then
just as suddenly as they came,
they left

lights off
windows closed
doors locked

Leaving nothing there

but a single
well-loved
chair

lonely

undiscovered

in a house
once filled
with love

but now
not even the
memories engrained
in the rotting wood
can ever be
recovered

A lonely chair
sits
in the corner
of the room
legs rotting
as puddles of damp
soak into the forgotten wood
and the sad smell of mould
permeates the air

Xanthe Turner

Bus stop

Time is ticking passed us

as we await our stop

Passing by the stations

where people pile up

Each of us on seperate journeys

yet we all share the trip

Lost in all our little worlds

in others' stories, just a blip

So come aboard with me

you don't need to stay for long

Everyone's a lyric

in each other's little song

Xanthe Turner

A Mandurian Story
By You

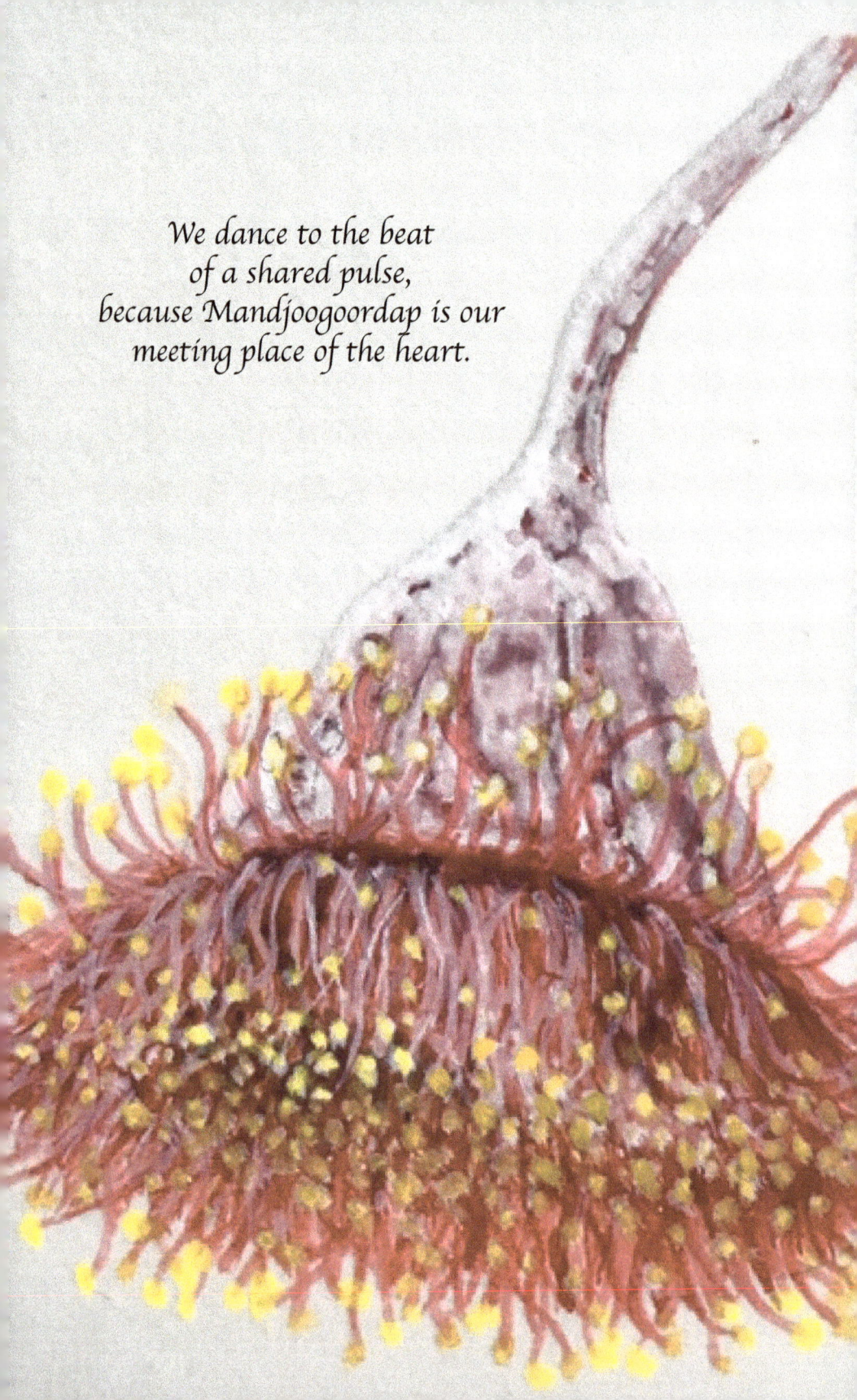

We dance to the beat
of a shared pulse,
because Mandjoogoordap is our
meeting place of the heart.

www.ingramcontent.com/pod-product-compliance
Lightning Source LLC
Chambersburg PA
CBHW062113290426
44110CB00023B/2795